PROFOUND PROFANITY

EXERCISES IN VULGARITY FOR THE CRUDE COLORIST

Swearing Silently Series | Volume 3

(American & British English)

ADULT COLORING BOOKS

Copyright © 2016 by ACB | Adult Coloring Books
Printed in the United States of America
Published by ACB | Adult Coloring Books
ISBN 978-1-988245-23-2

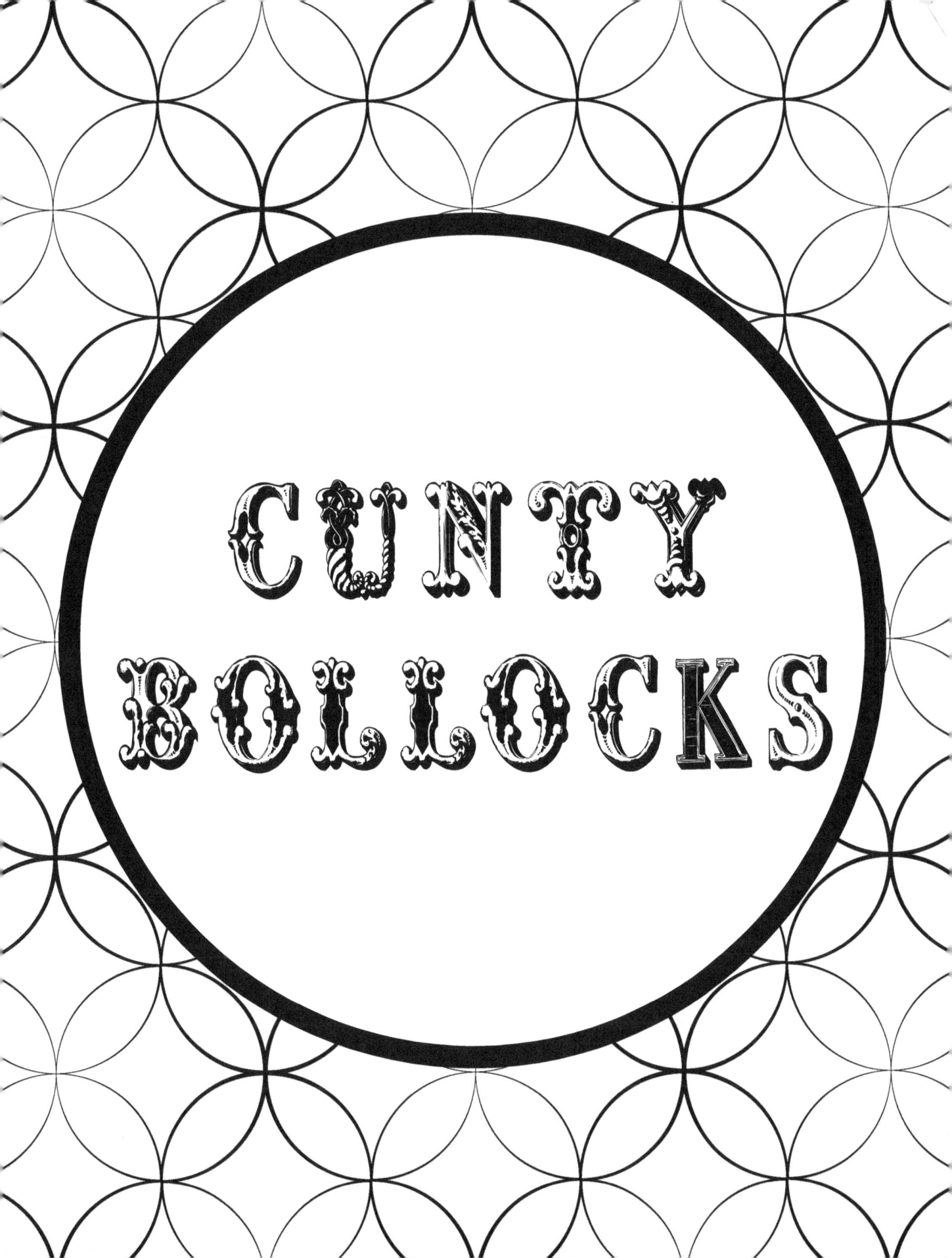

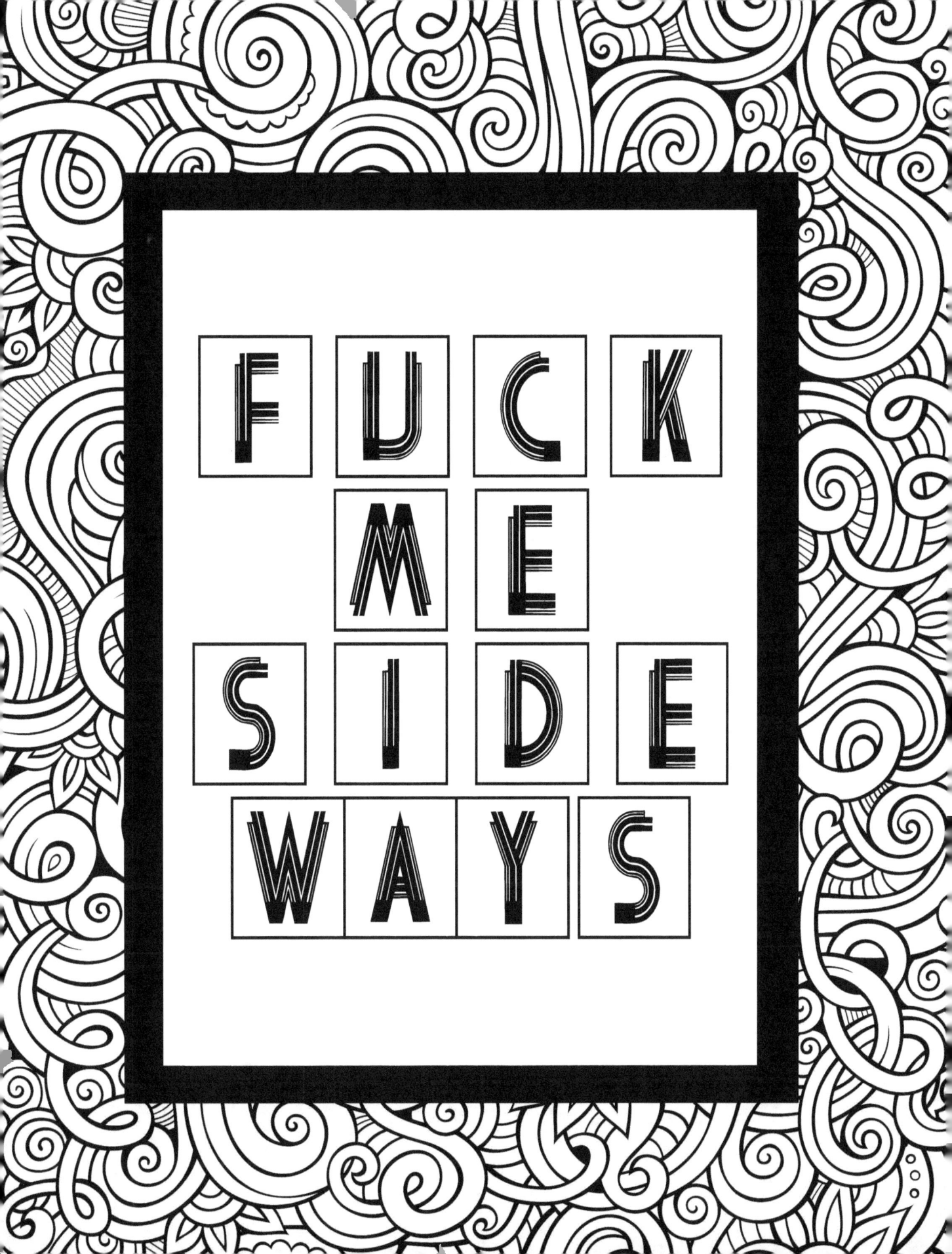

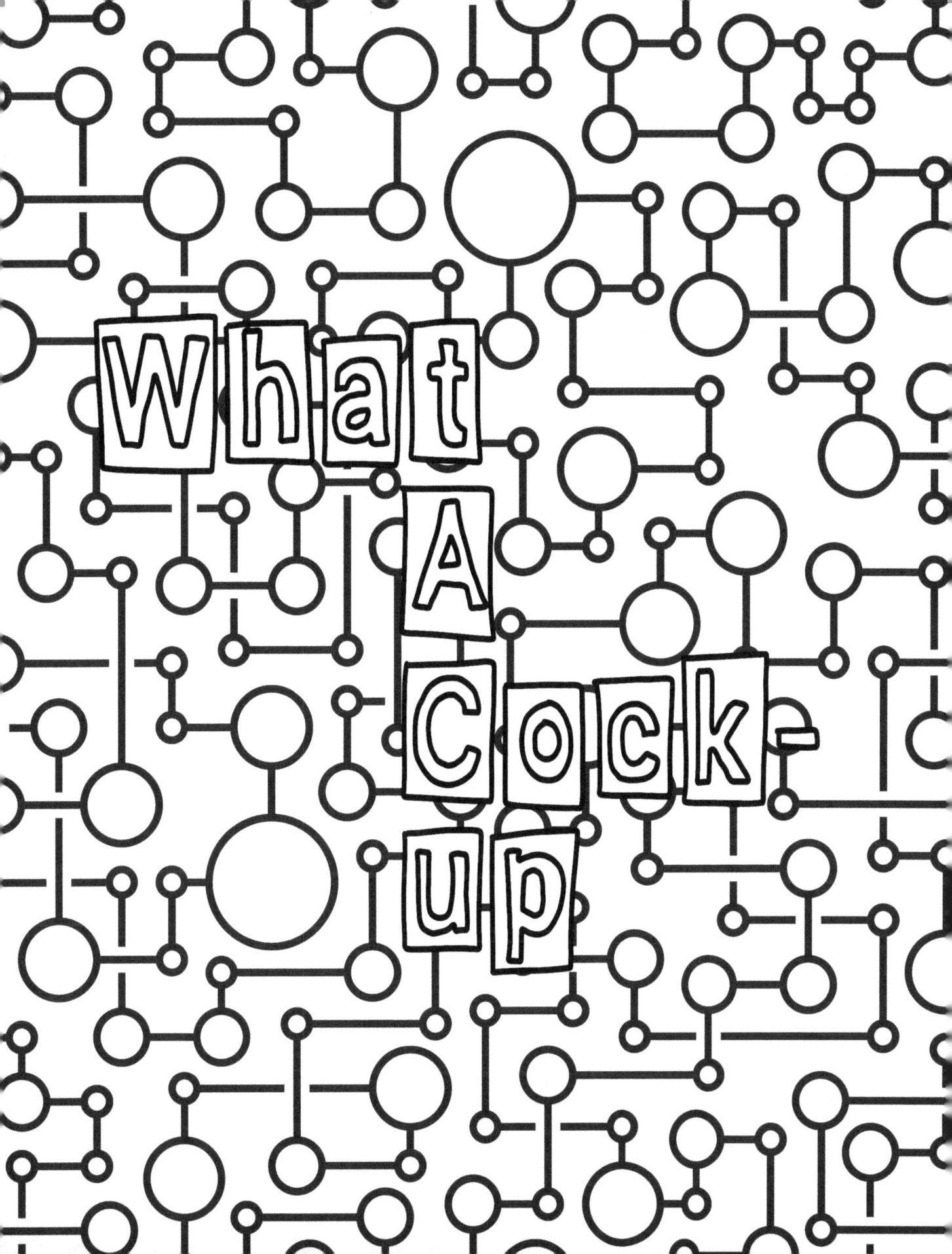

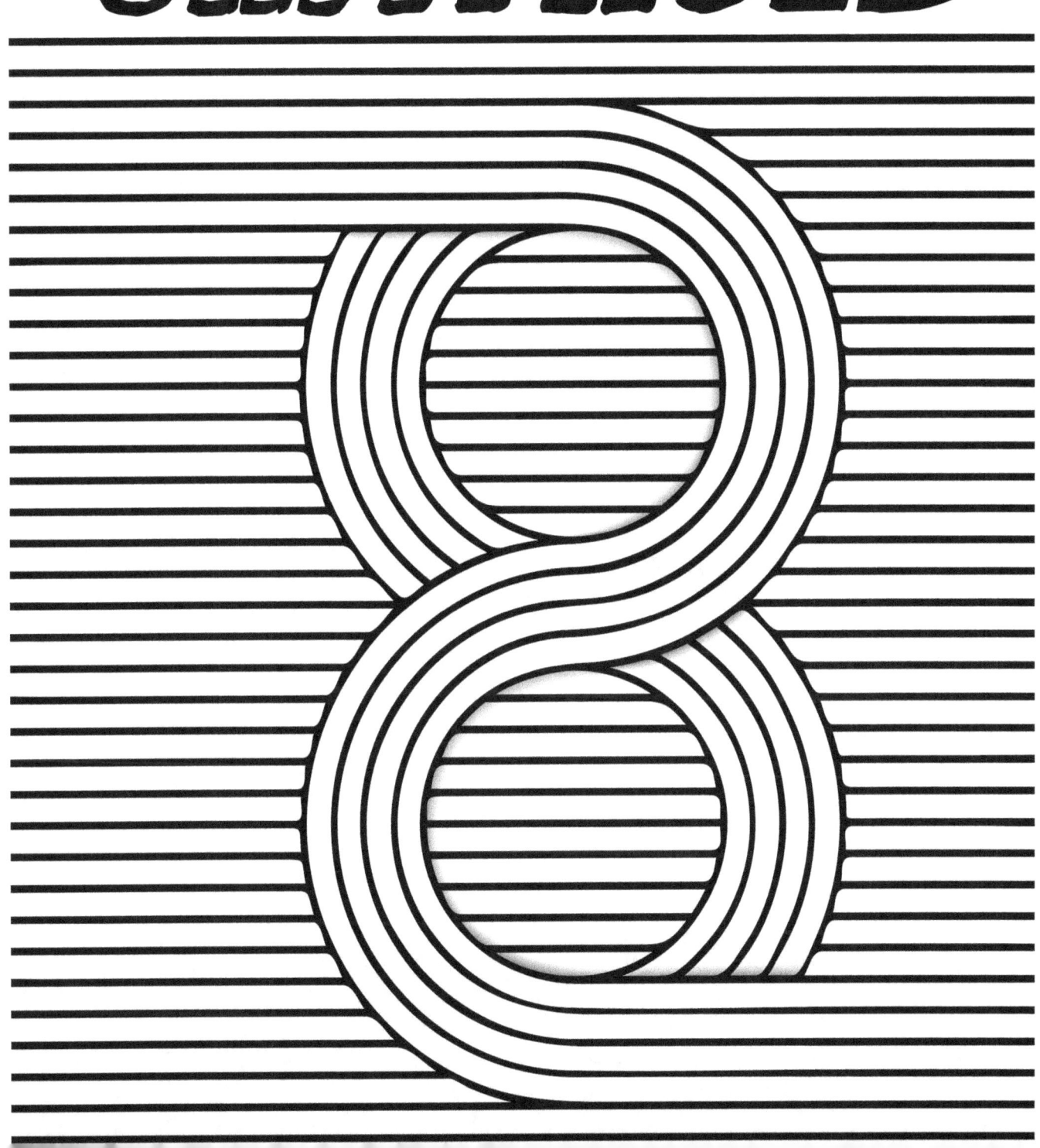

BAT SHIT CRAZY!!!!

PUSSY

JERK ASS

DAWN

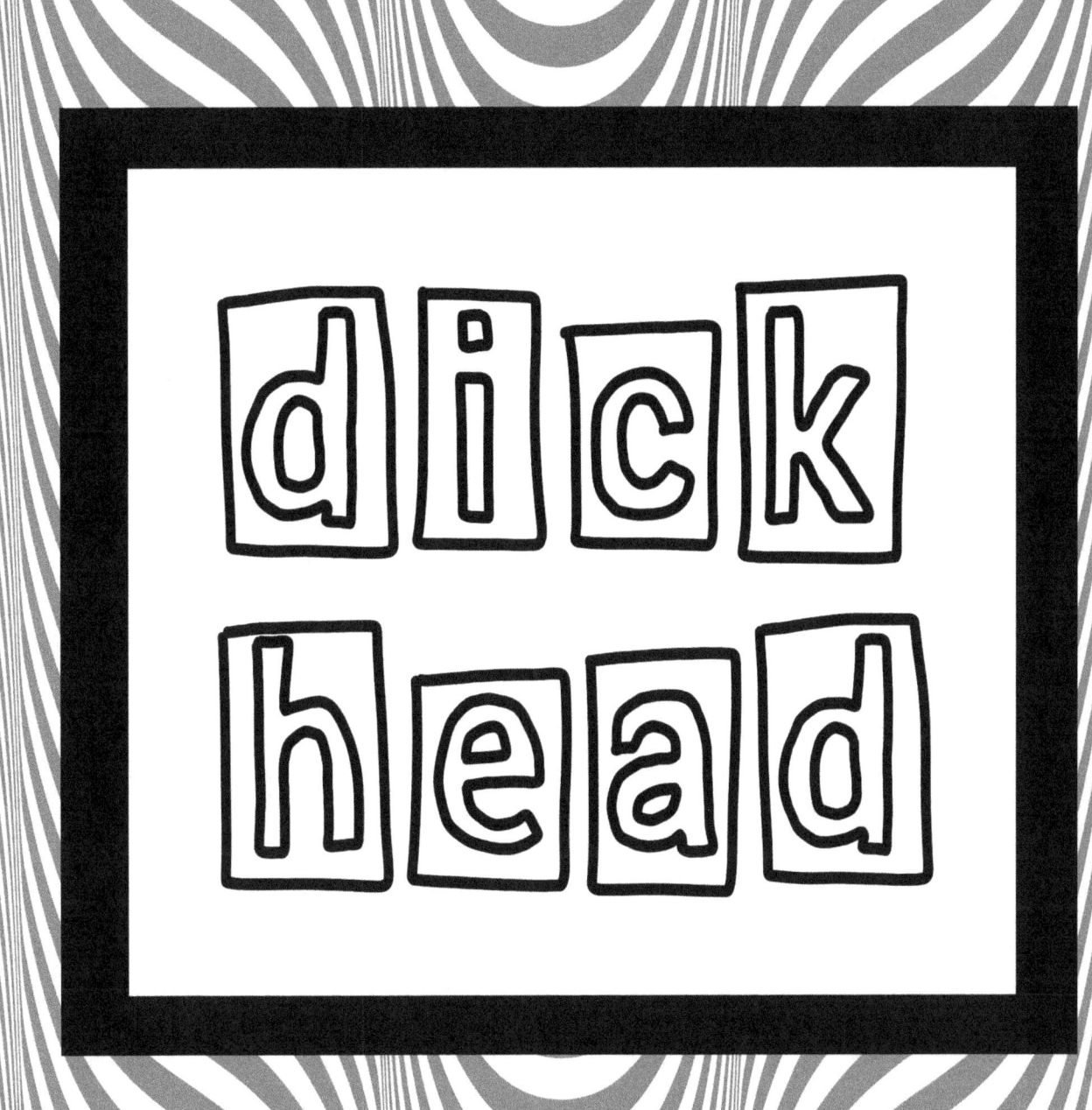

BITCH

ACB
ADULT COLORING BOOKS

Check out the other books in the Swearing Silently series, containing the images within this book and more! Also have a look at our complete collection of books, listed at amazon.com/author/acbadultcoloringbooks

Slang Slinger - American edition with 50 pages of swear words common to American English (ISBN 978-1988245126)

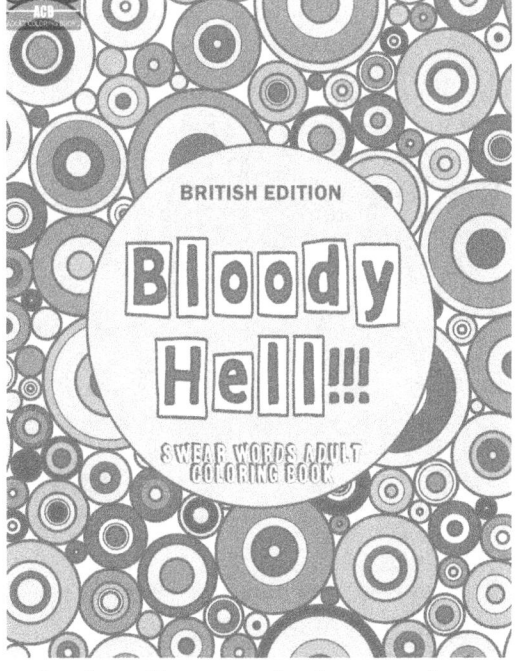

Bloody Hell!!! - British edition with 50 pages of swear words common to British English (ISBN 978-1988245201)

www.ingramcontent.com/pod-product-compliance
Lightning Source LLC
Chambersburg PA
CBHW081431070526
44586CB00020B/2553